Keep it Simple

MY 1ST LEARNING BOOK

THE FLASH CARD BOOK
(NO PICTURES)

Alphabets
(Uppercase & Lowercase)

Colors

Numbers

1-20

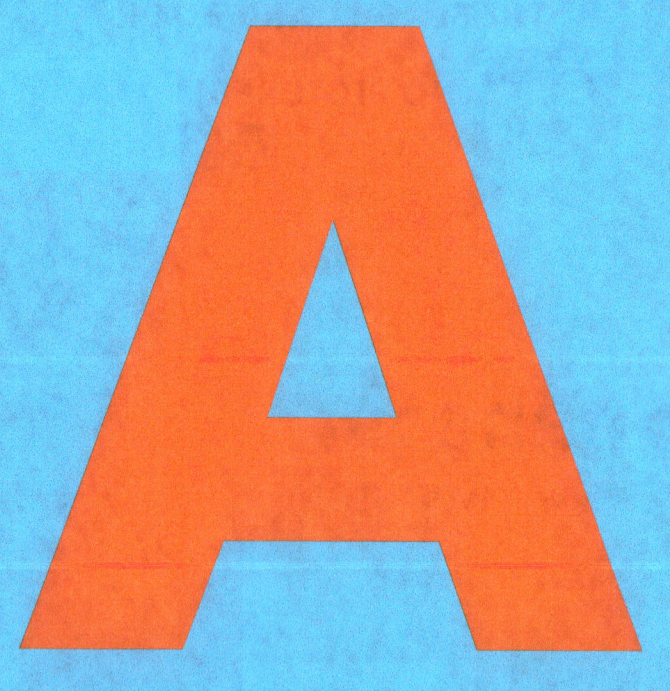

a

B

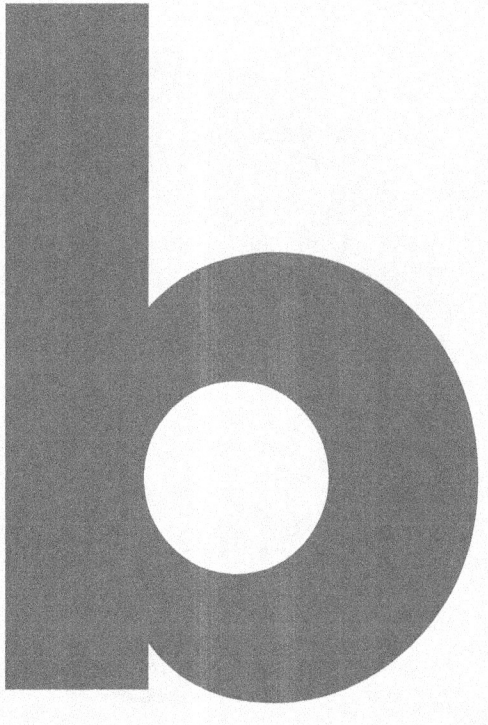

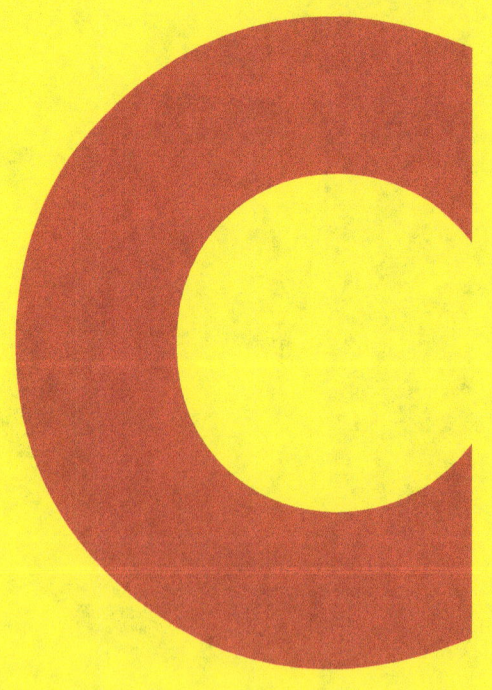

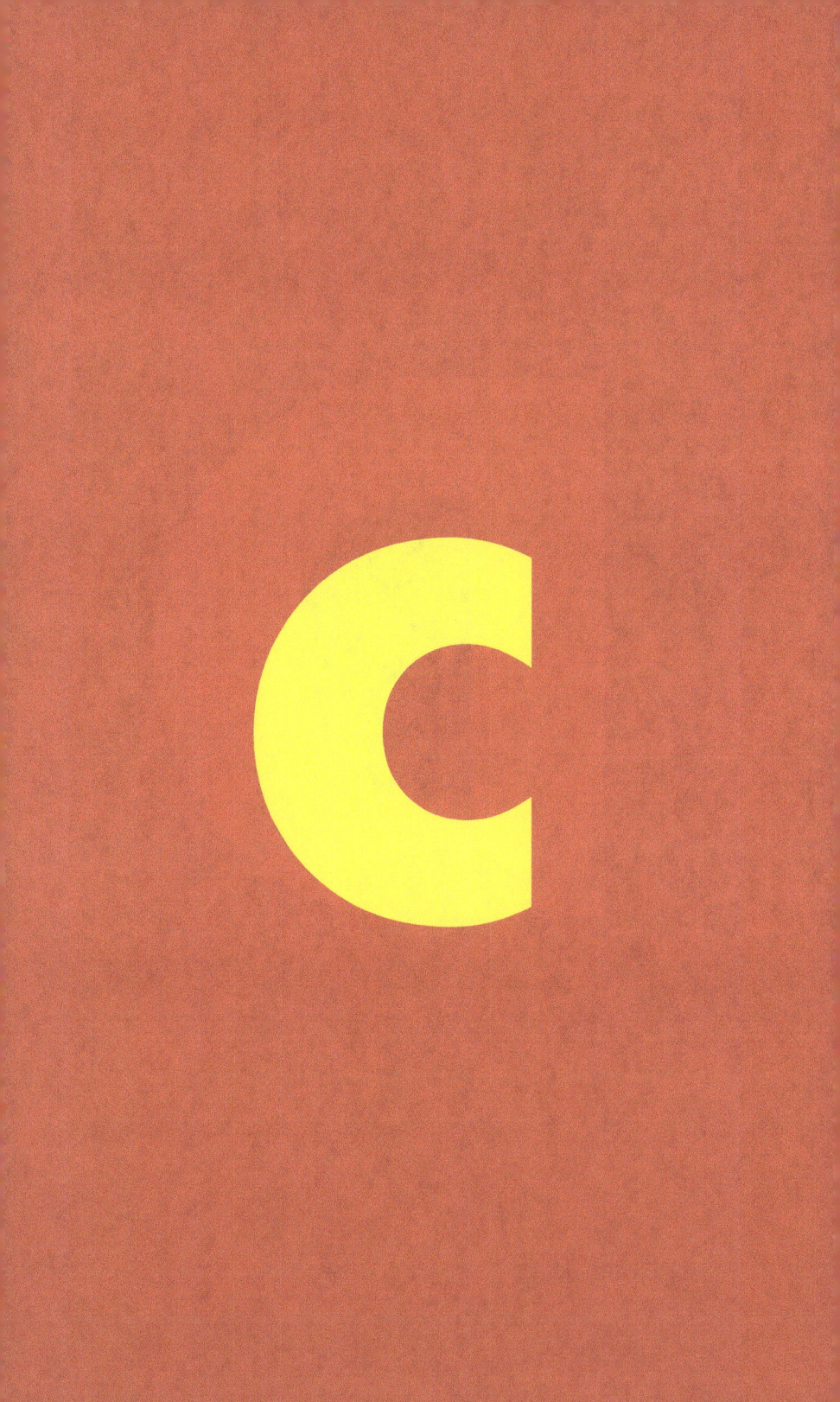

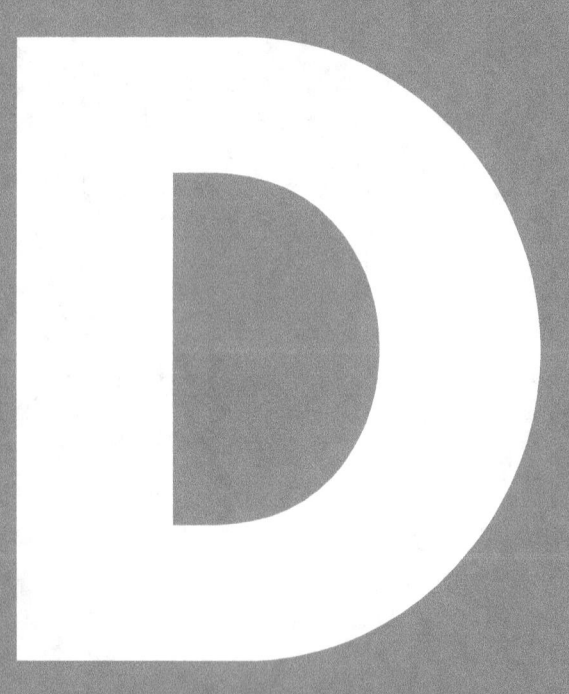

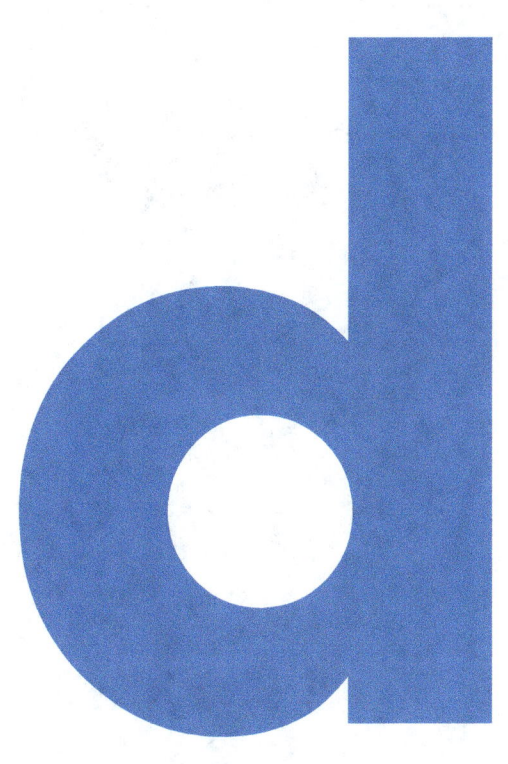

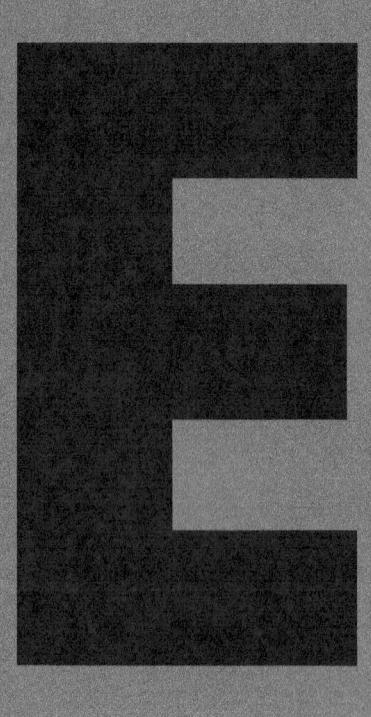

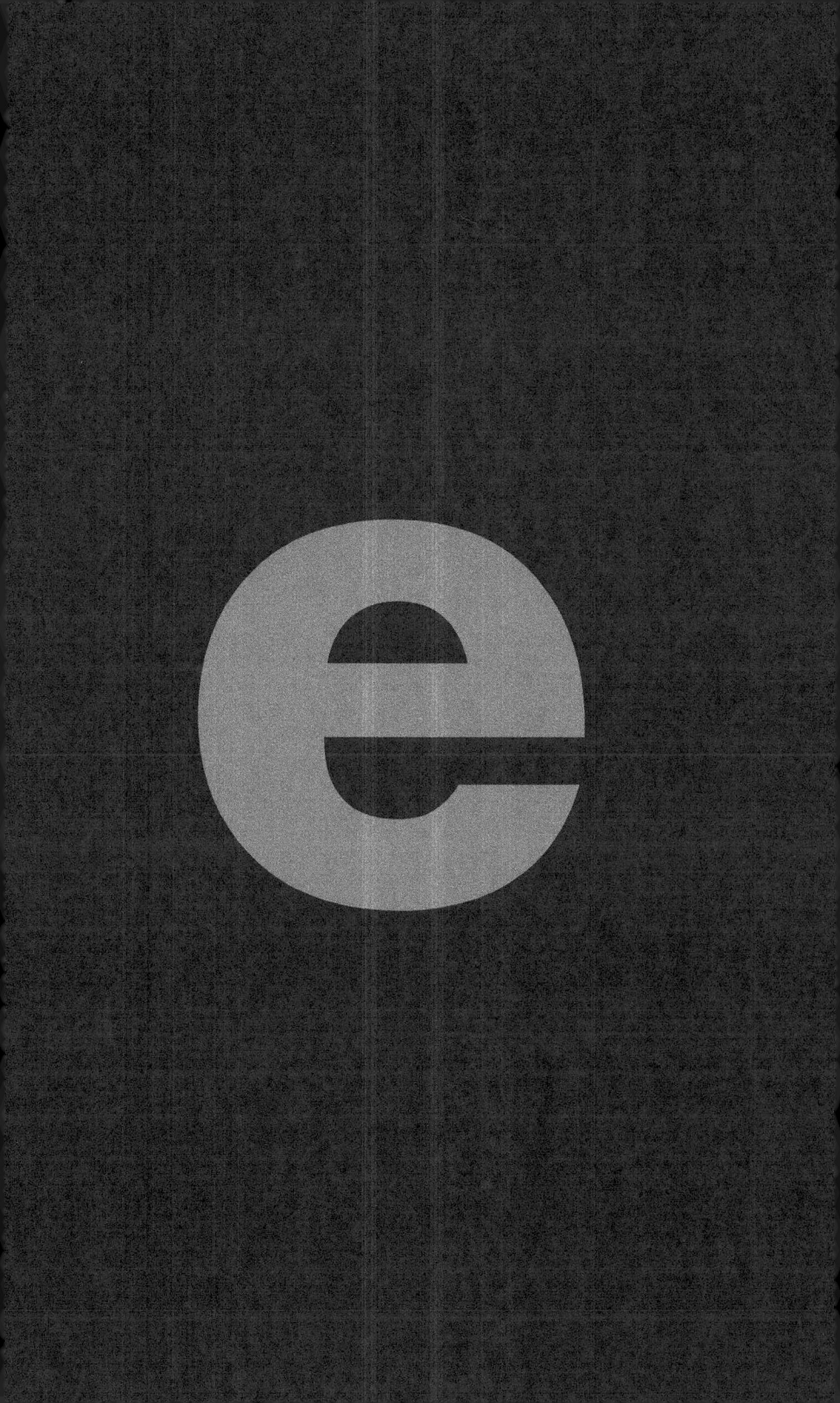

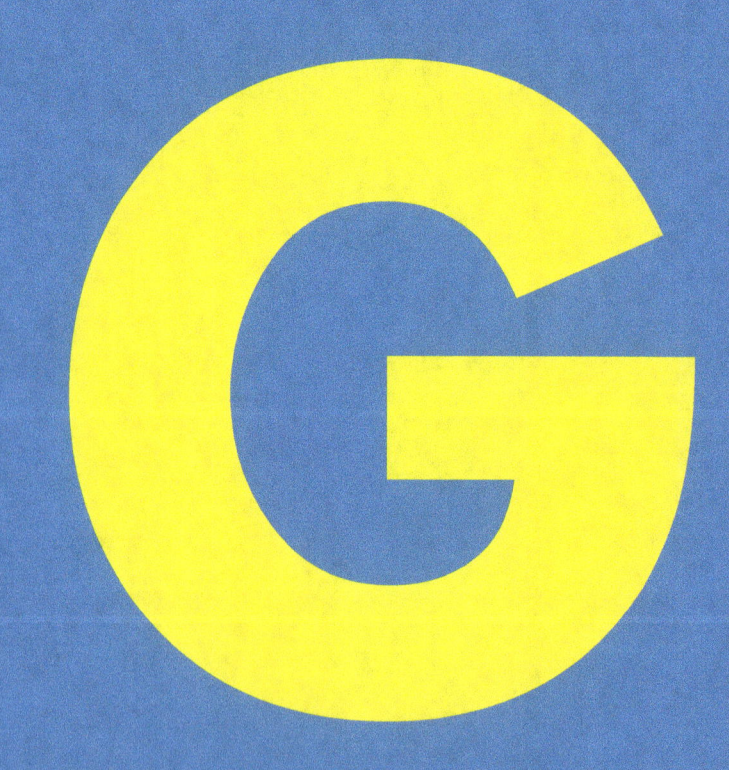

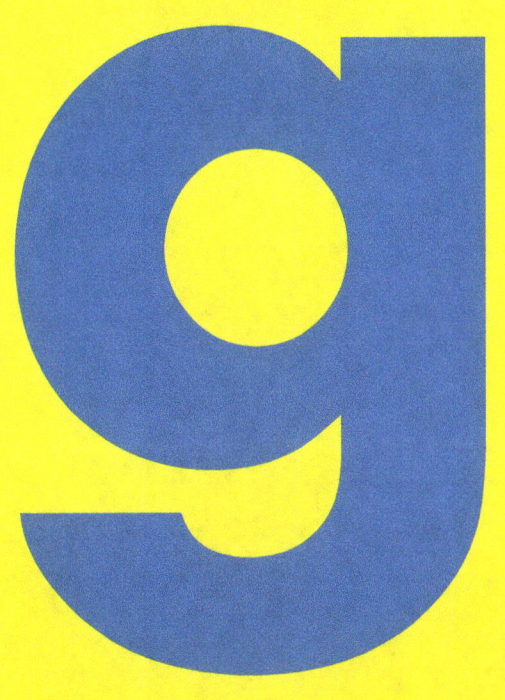

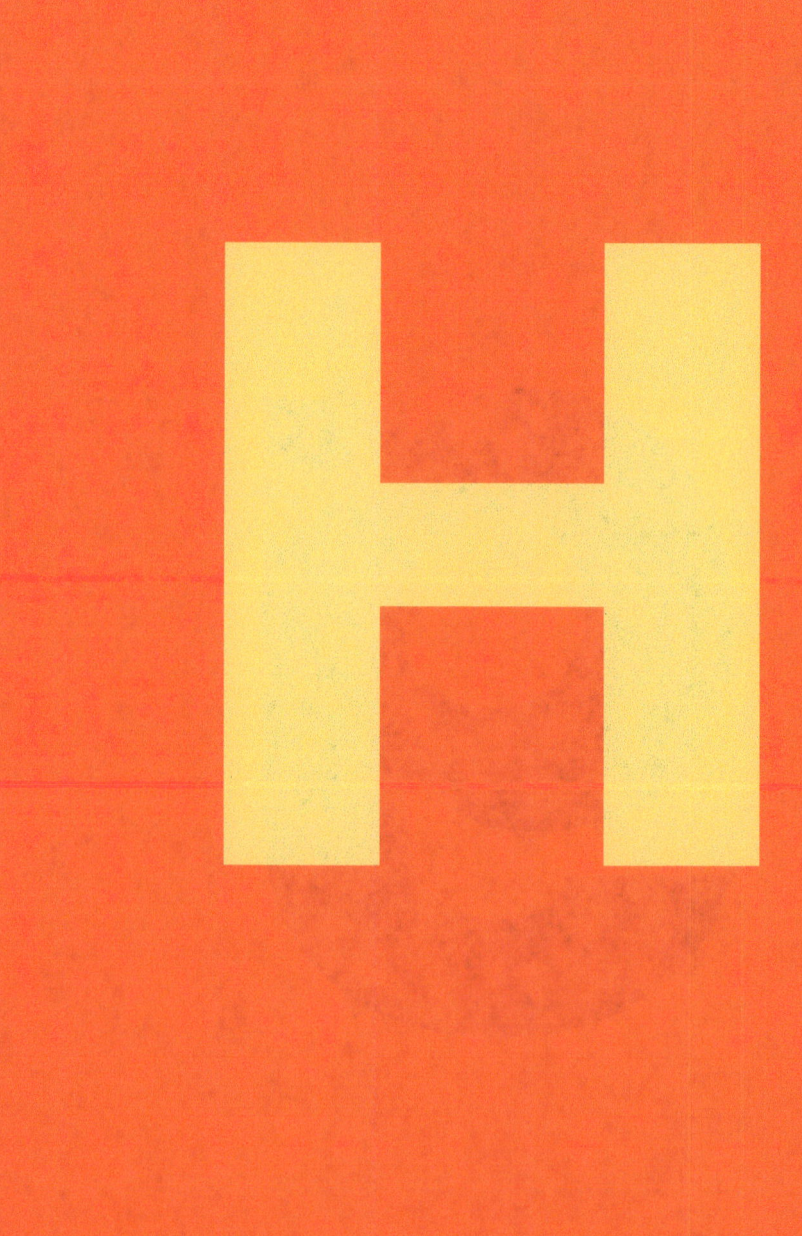

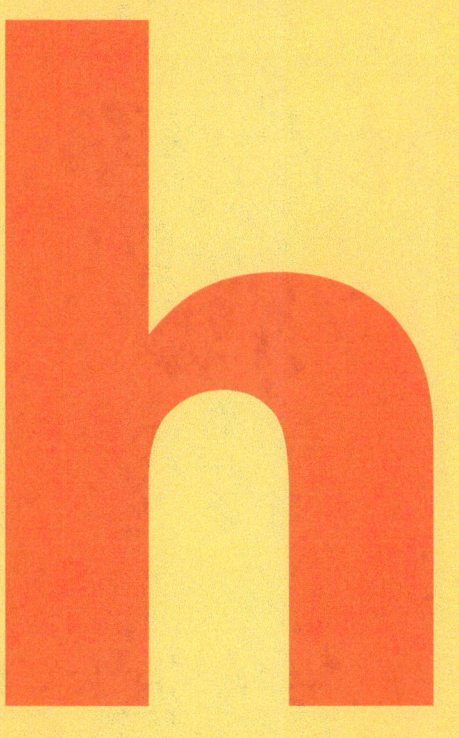

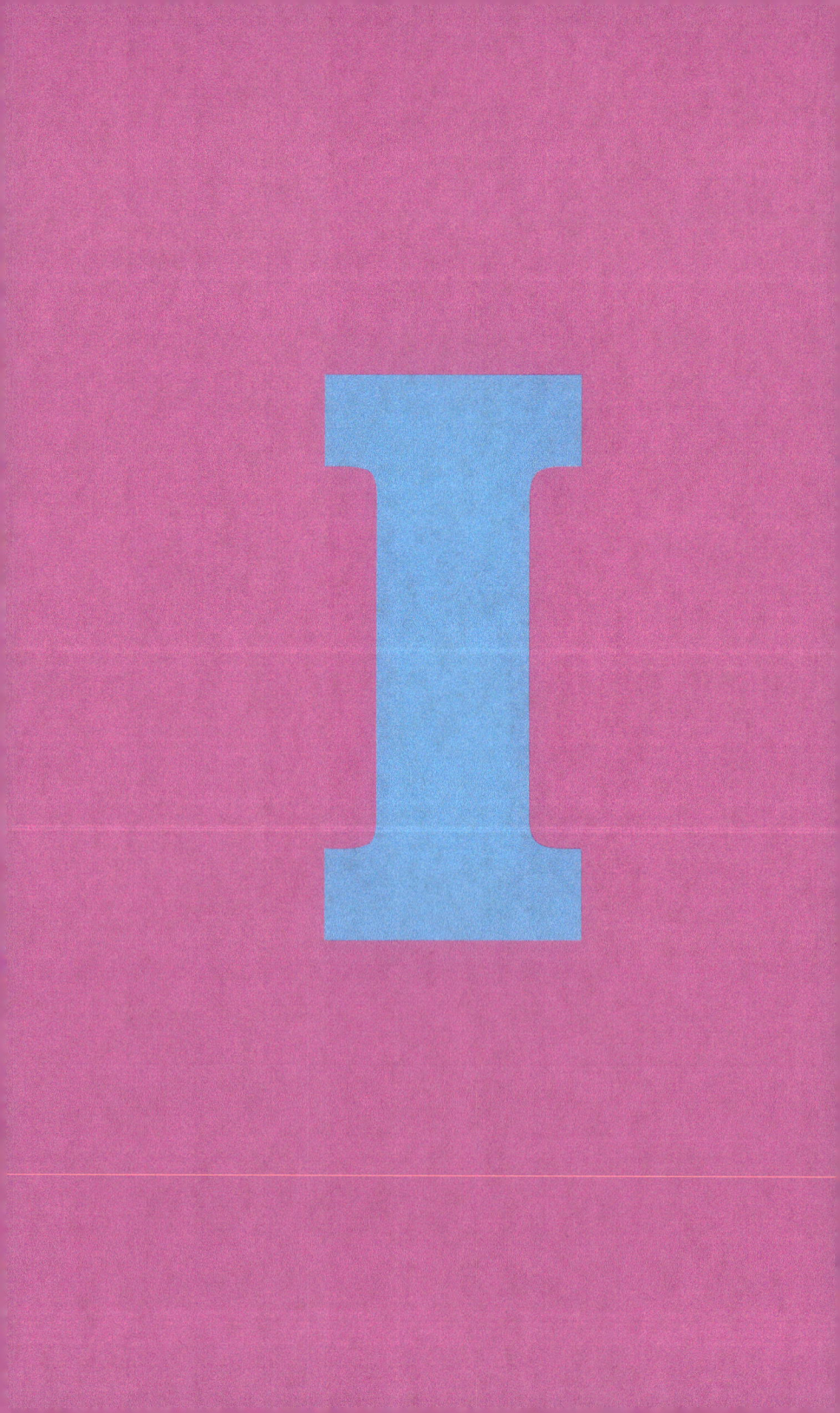

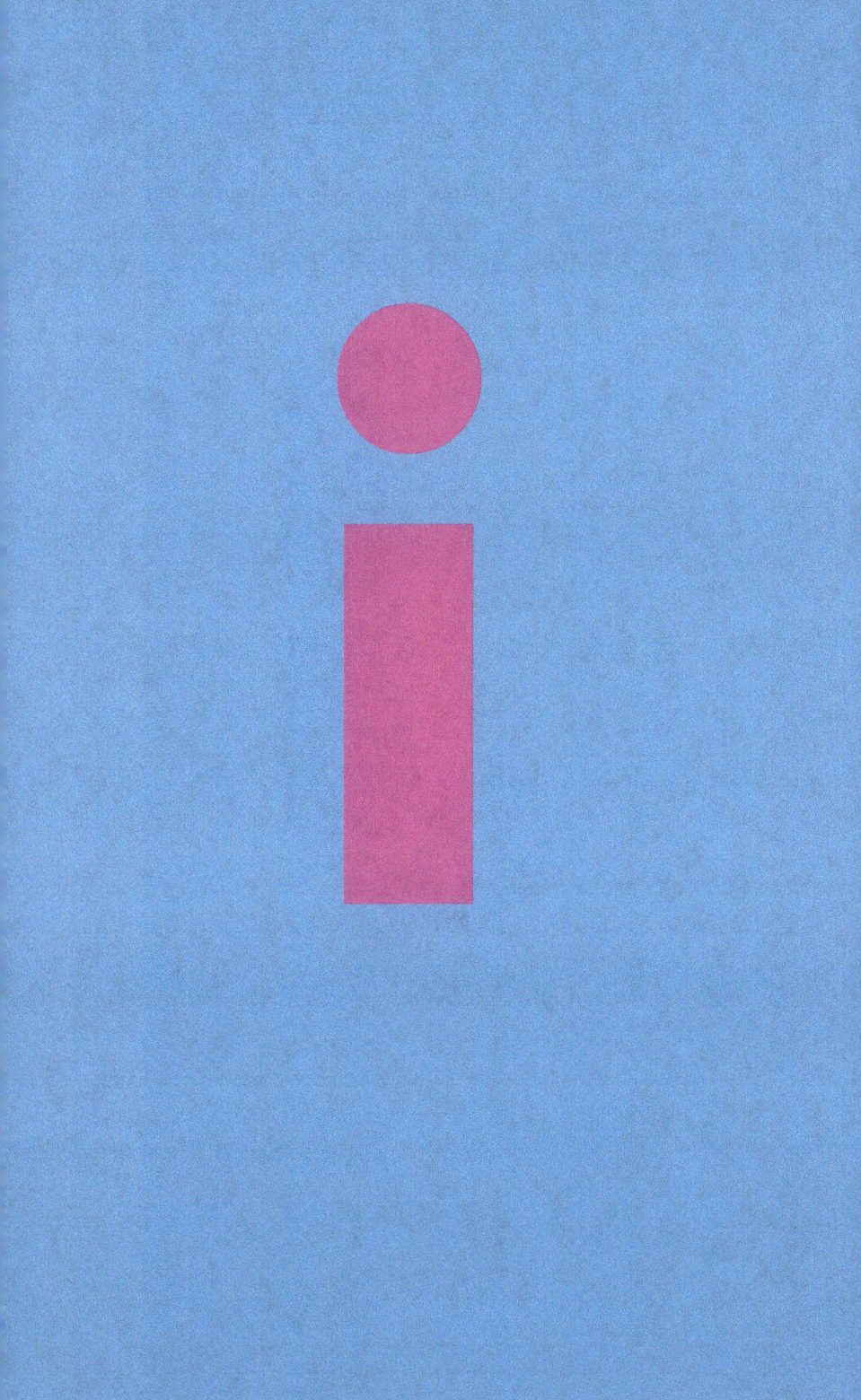

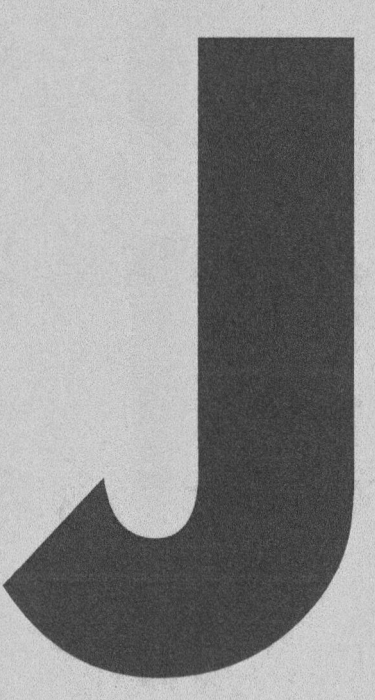

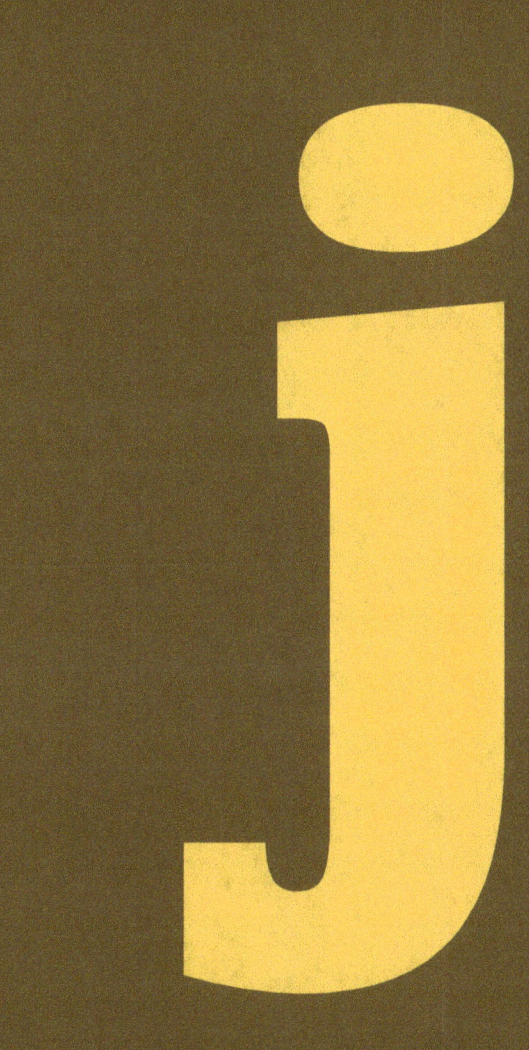

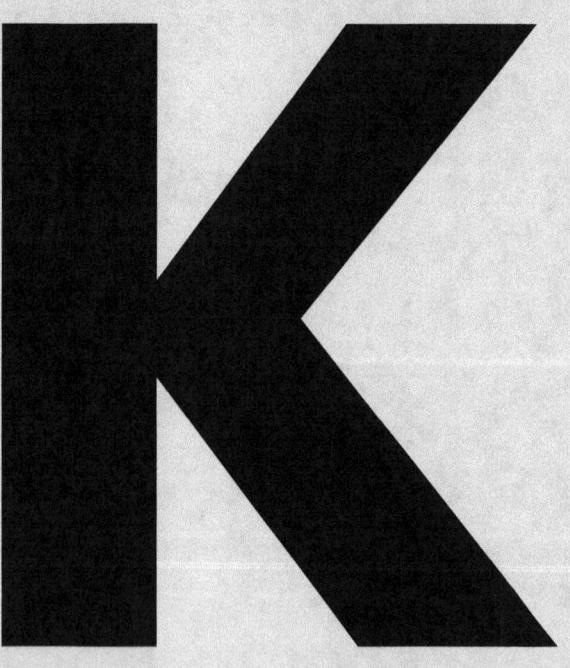

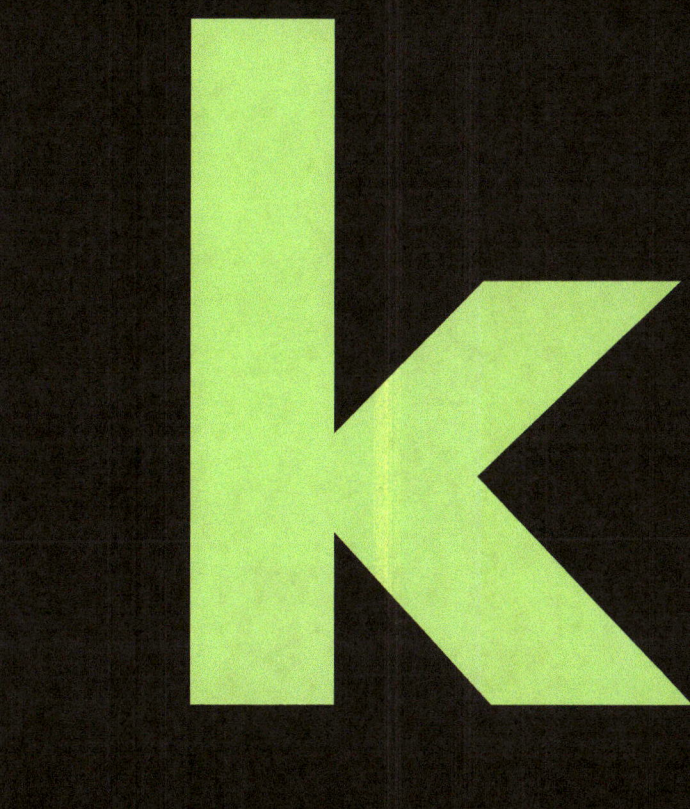

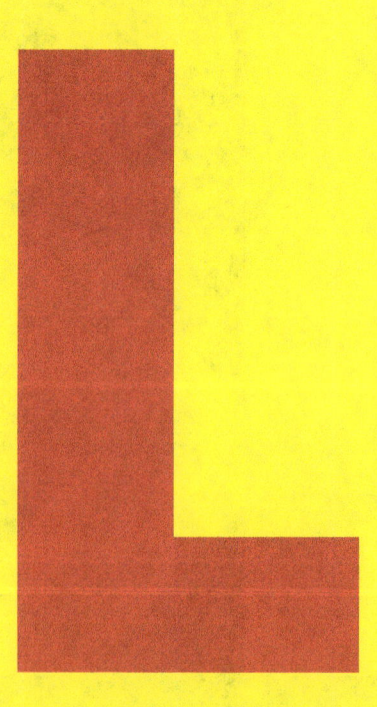

M

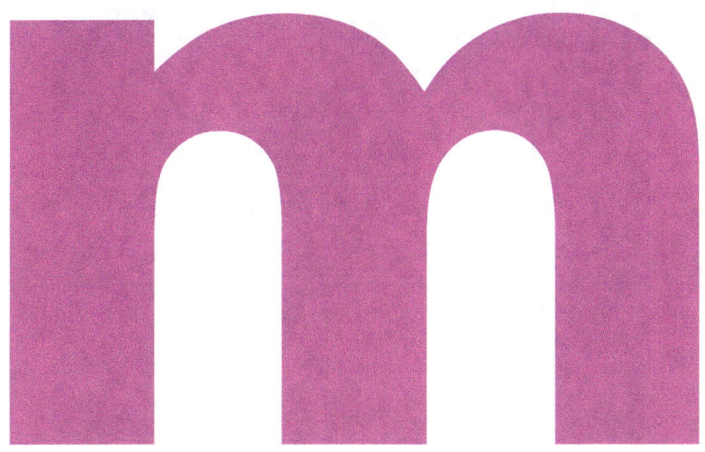

N

P

p

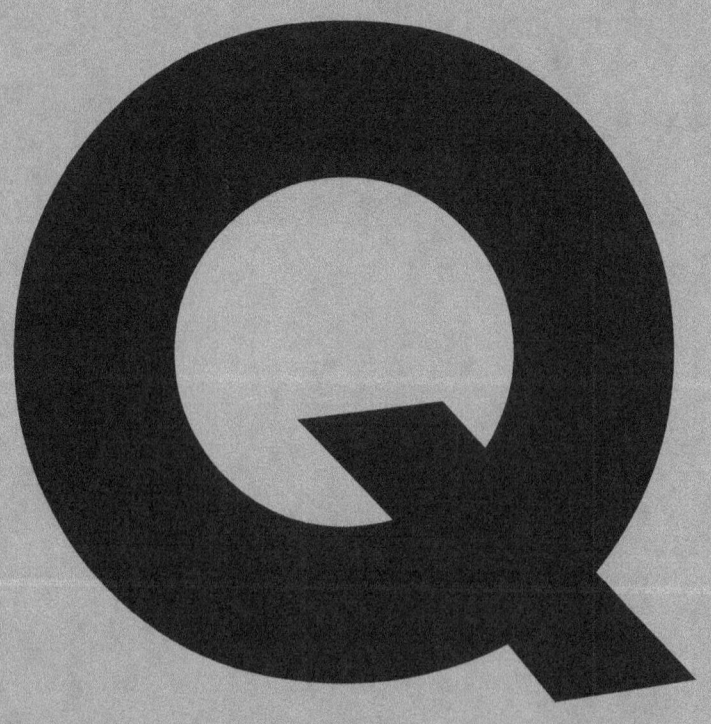

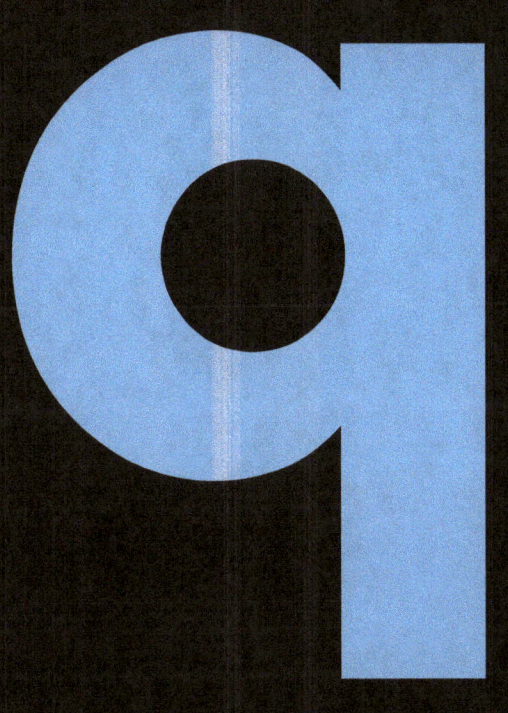

R

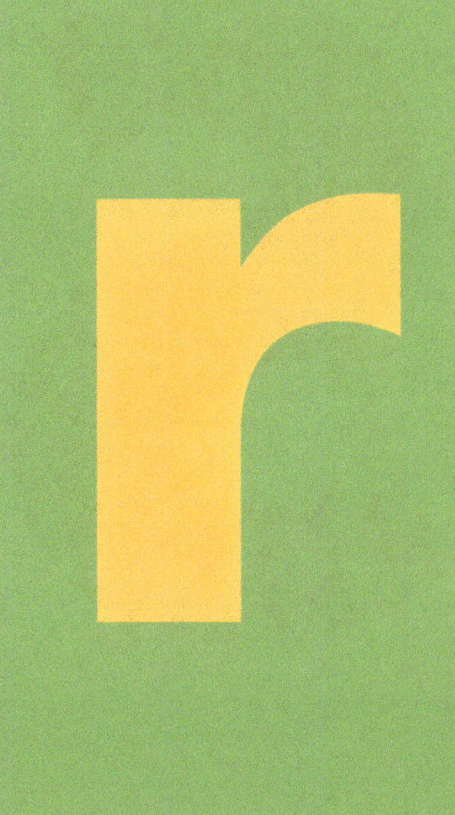

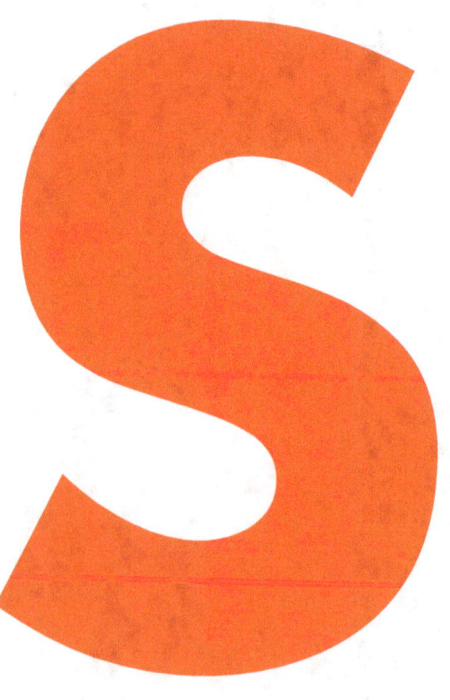

s

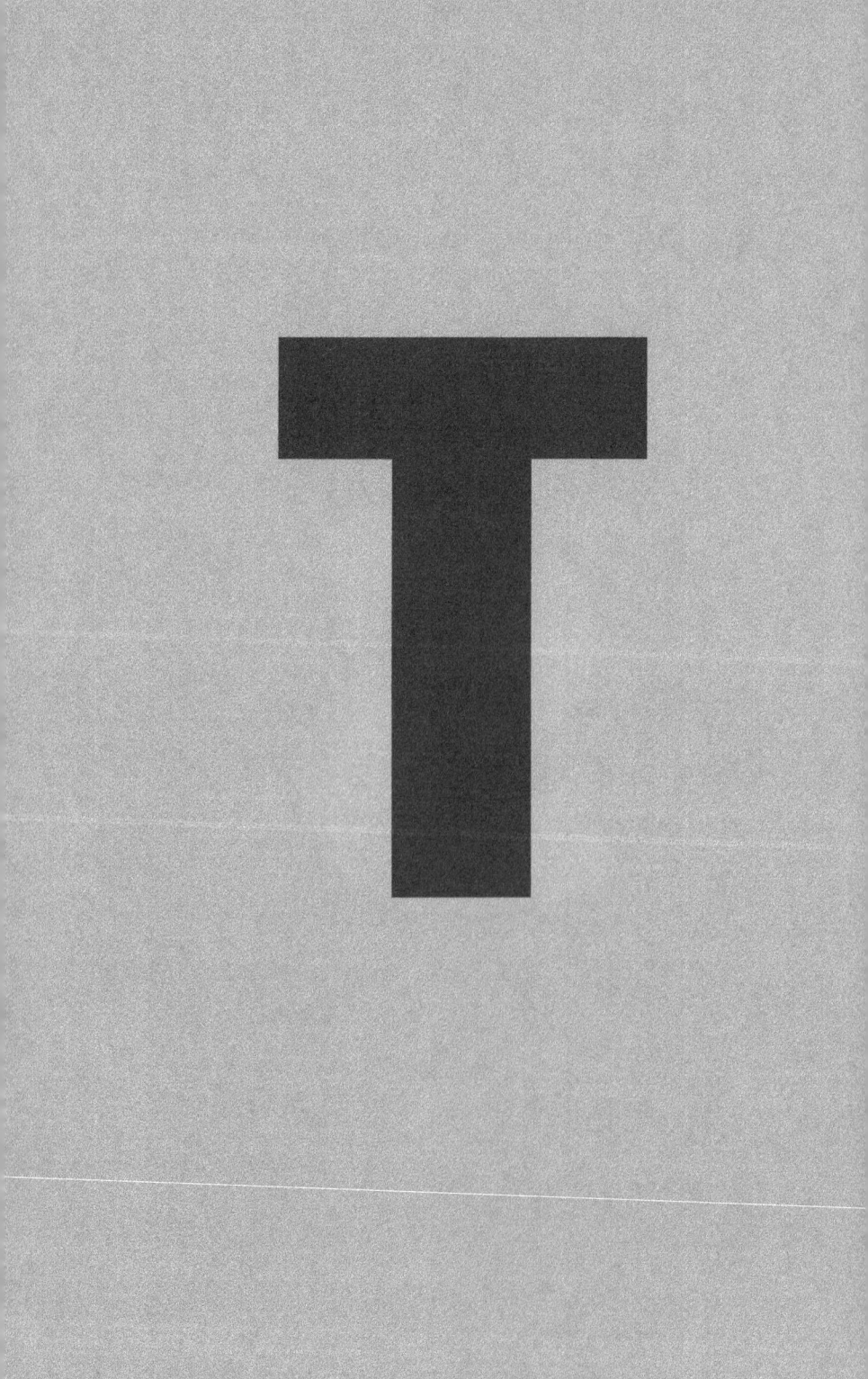

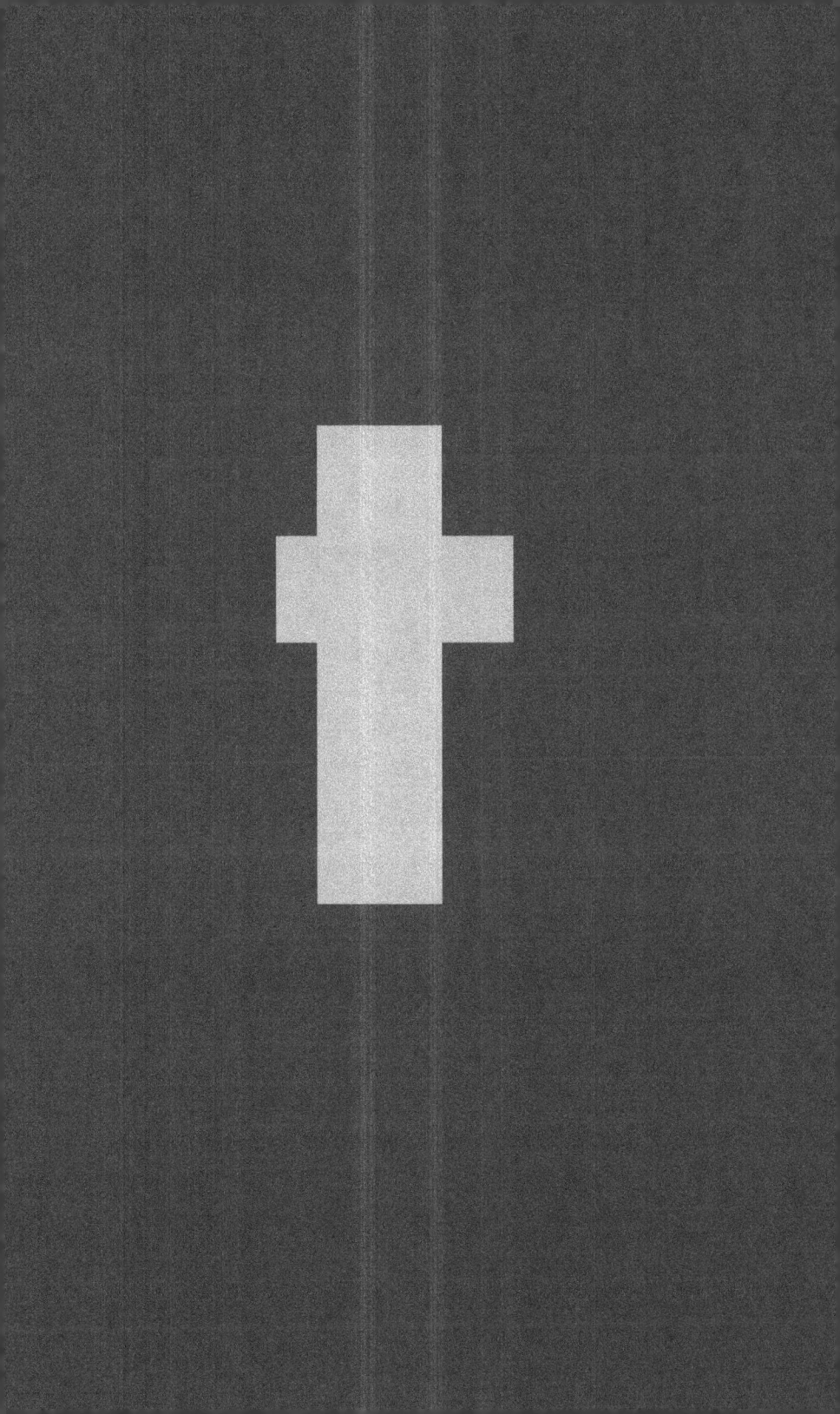

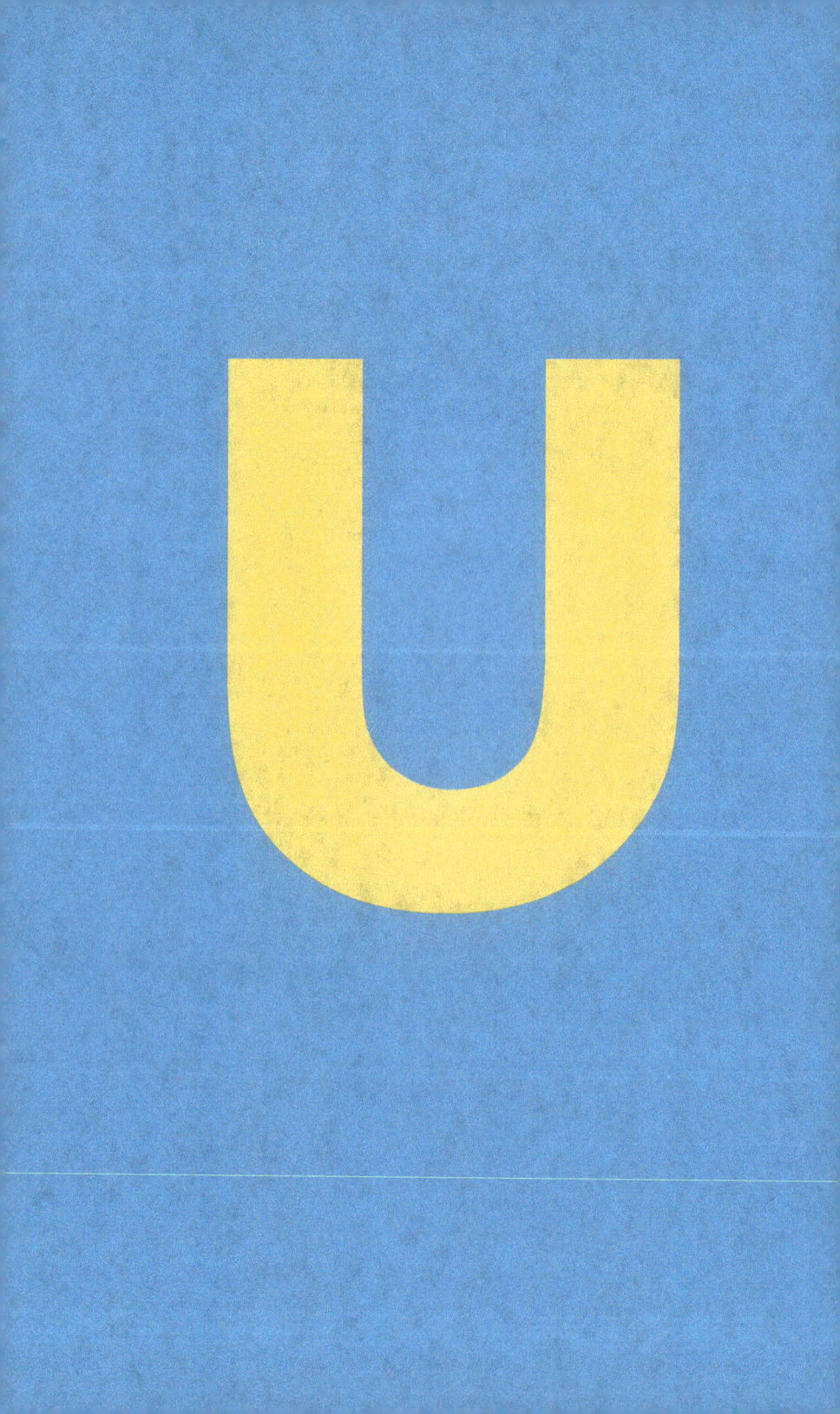

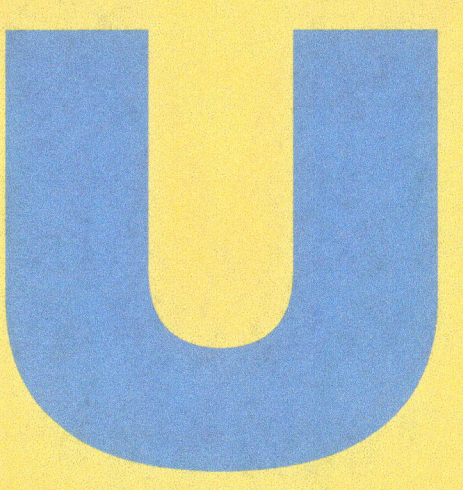

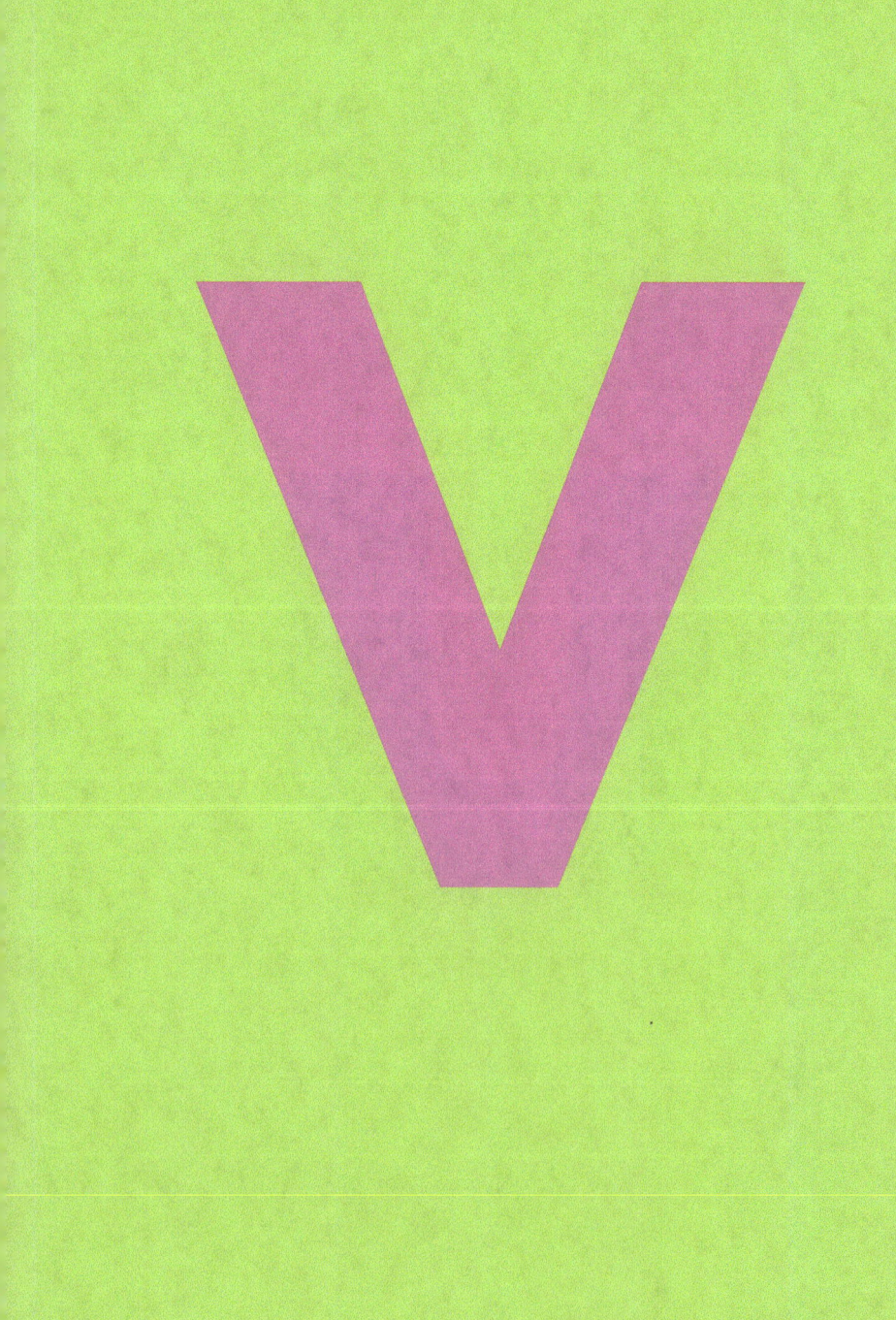

v

W

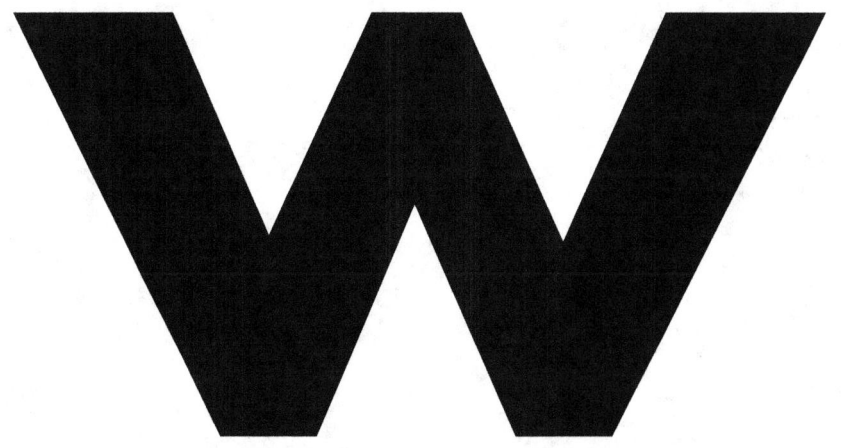

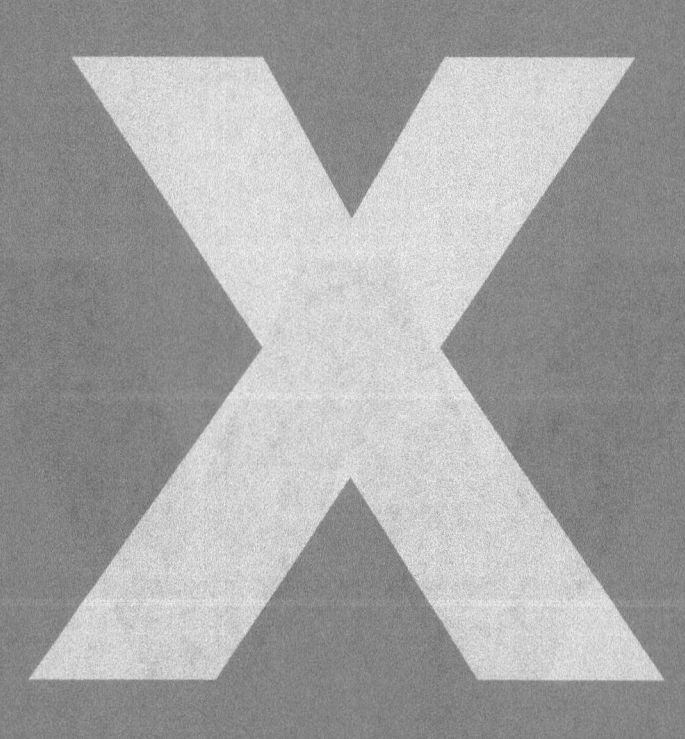

x

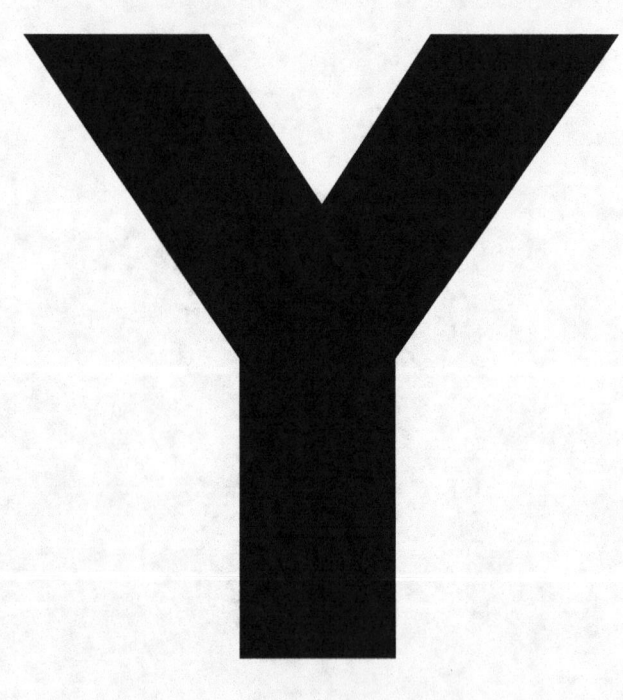

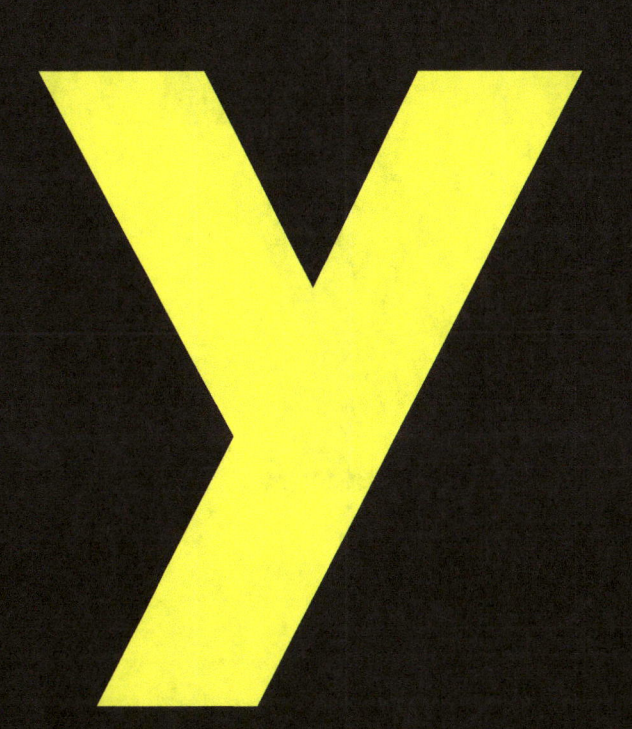

Z

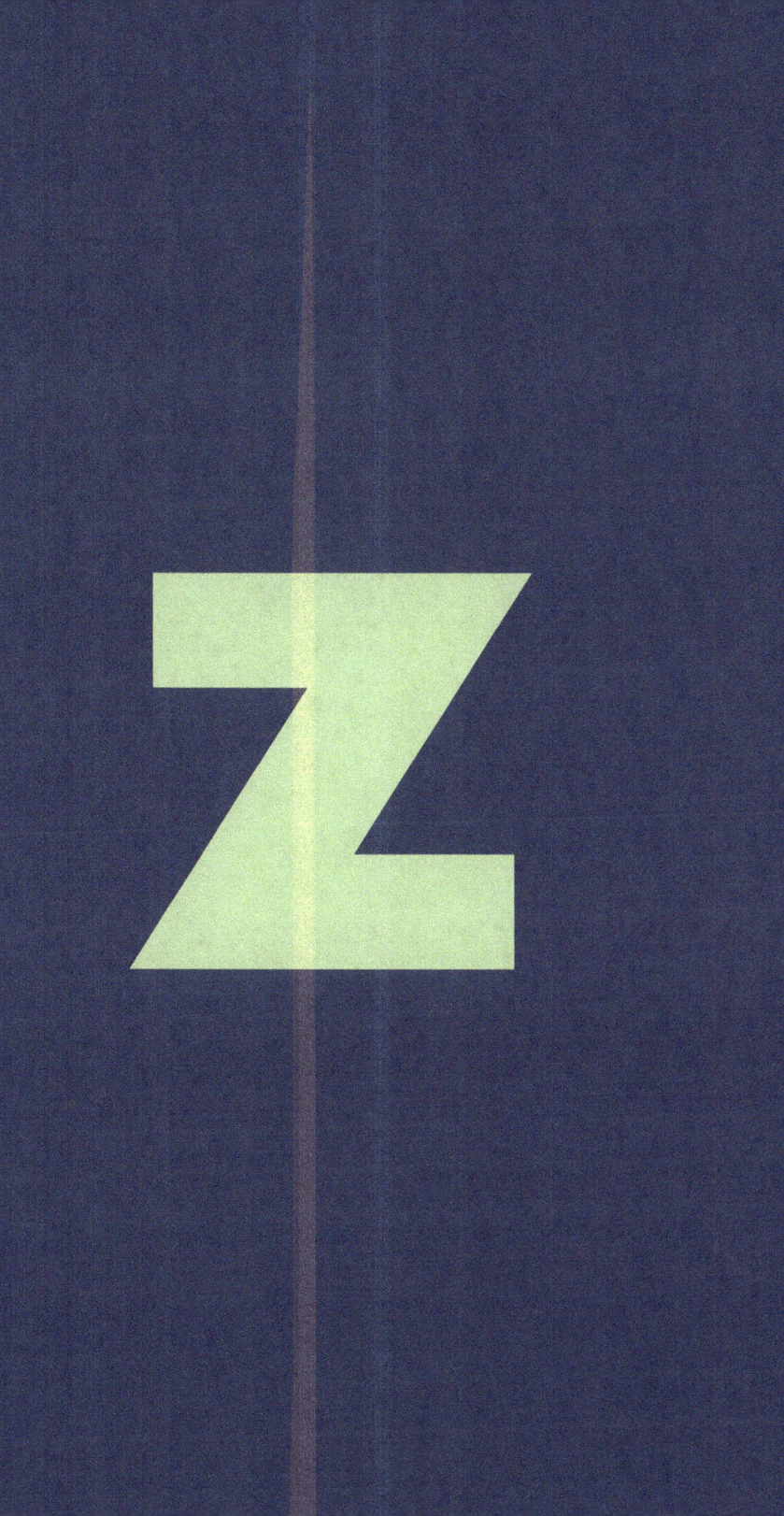

white

black

blue

red

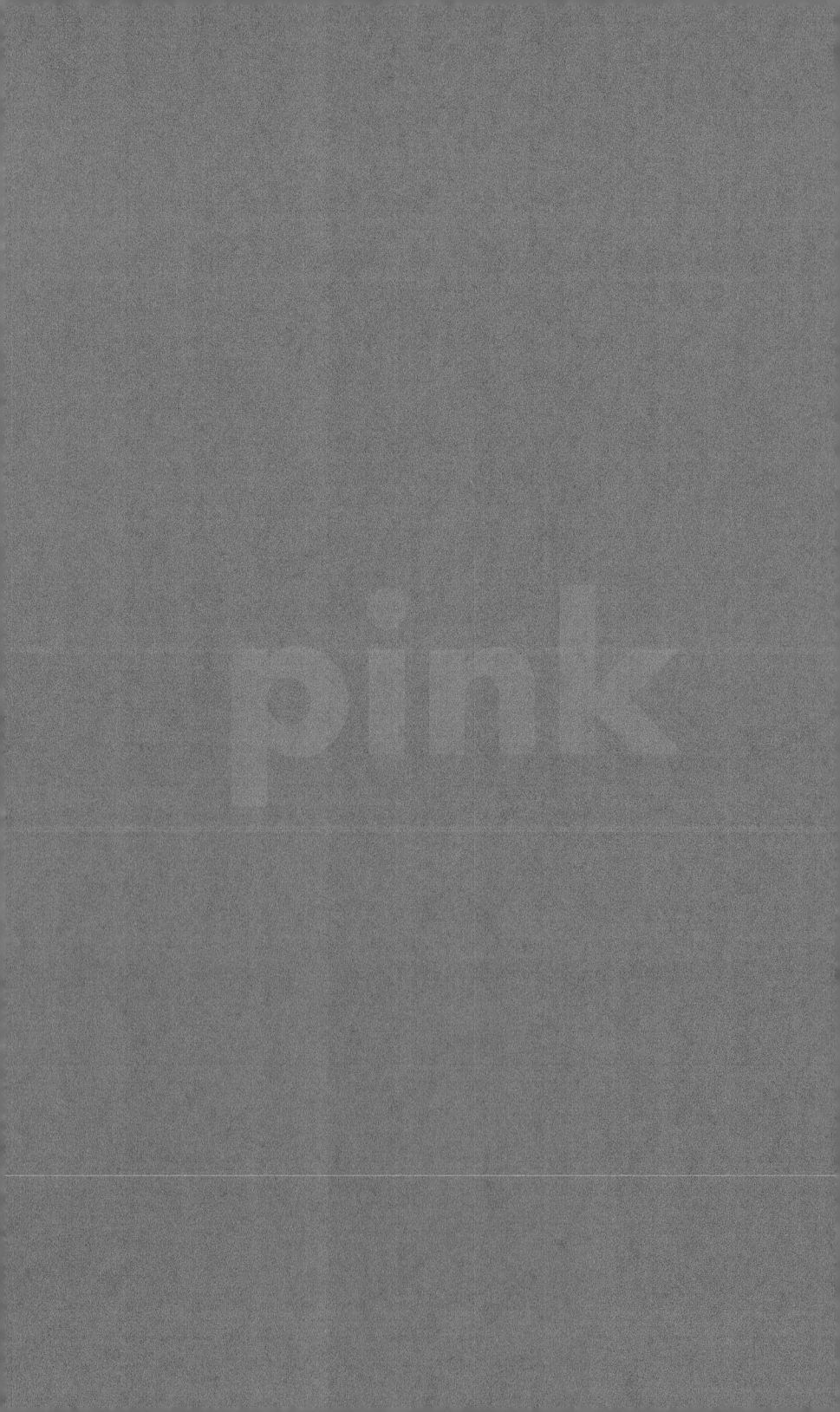

brown

gray

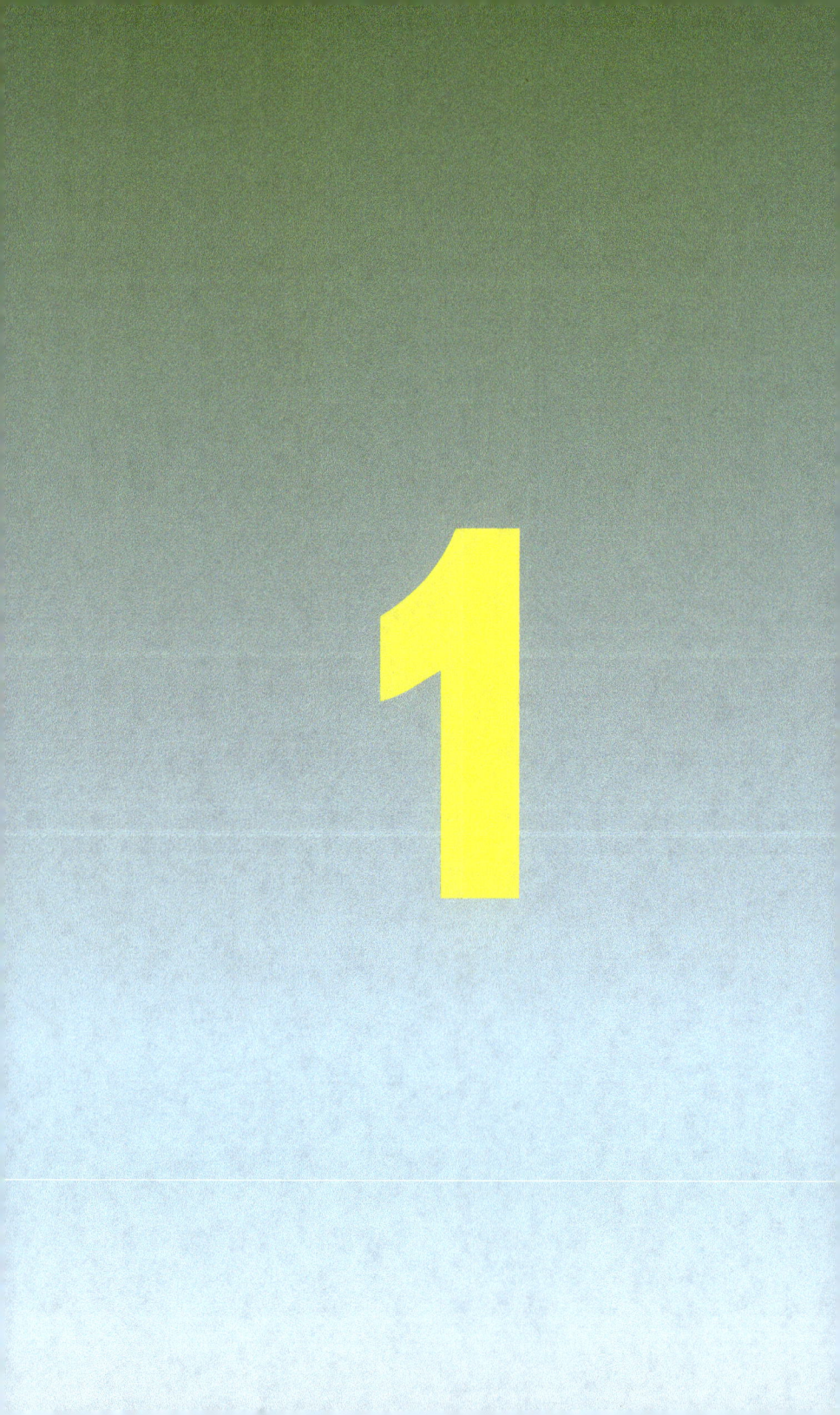

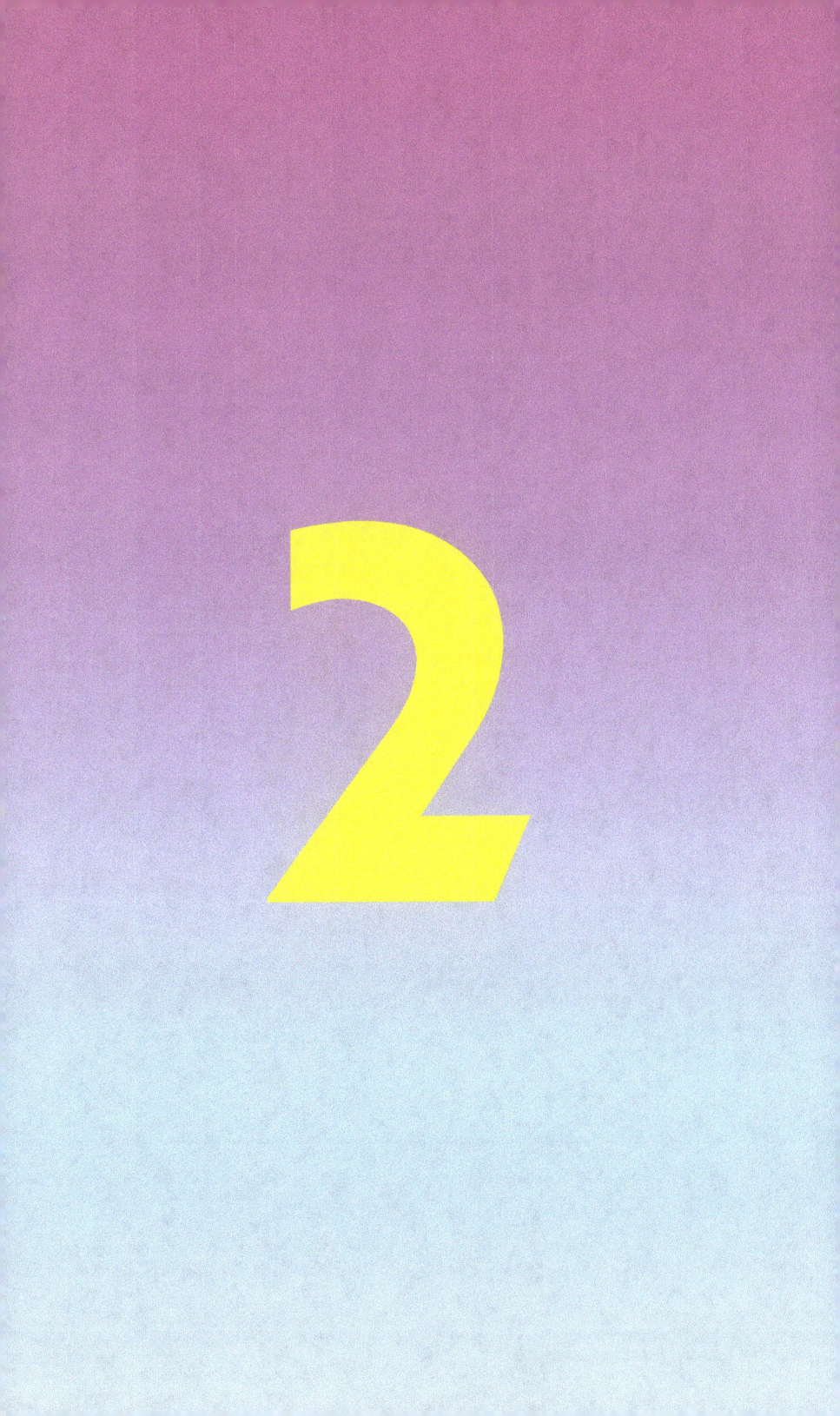

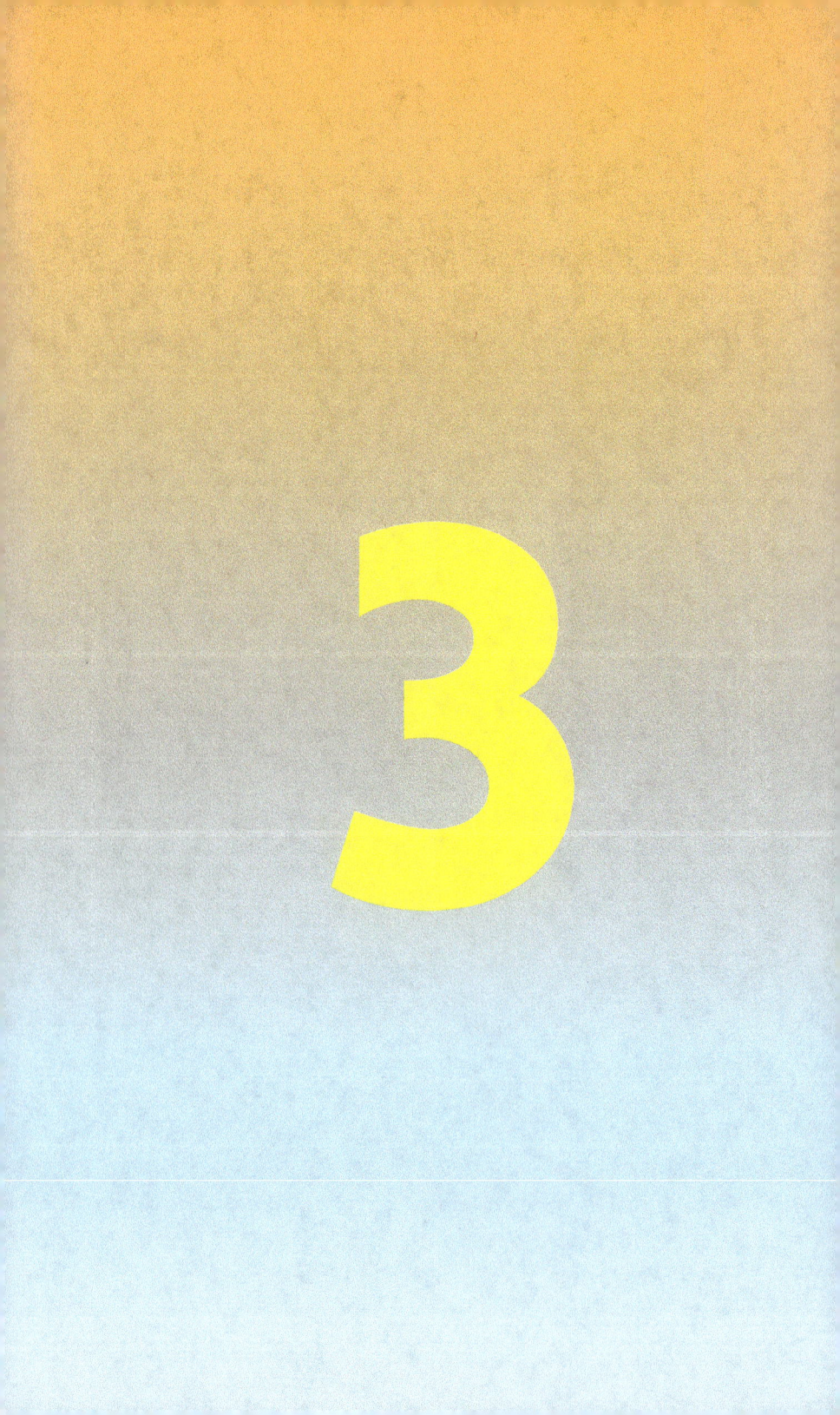

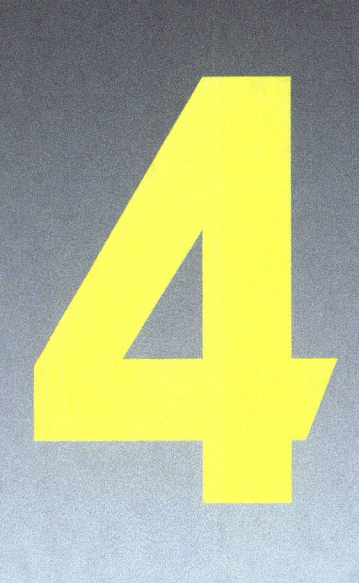

5

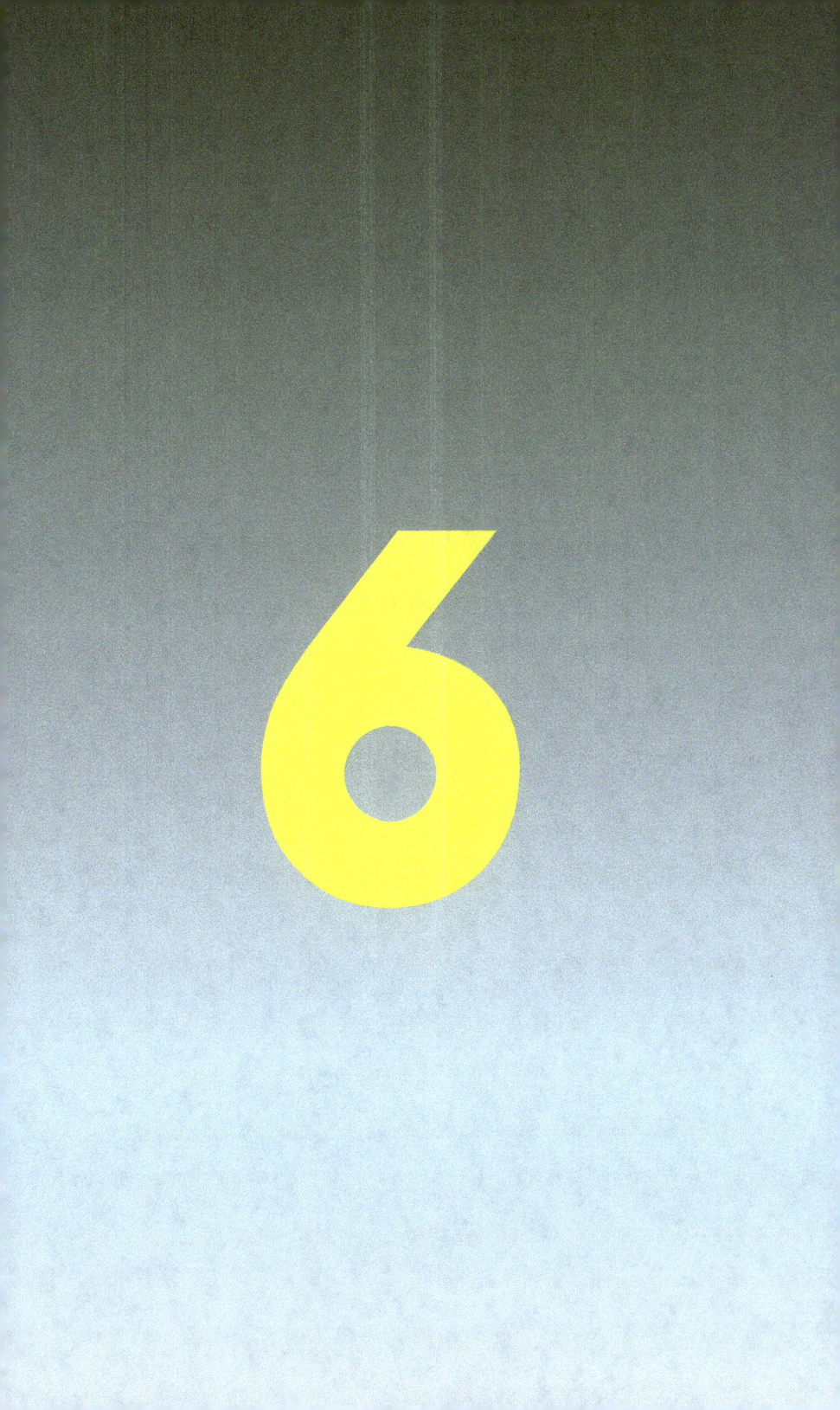

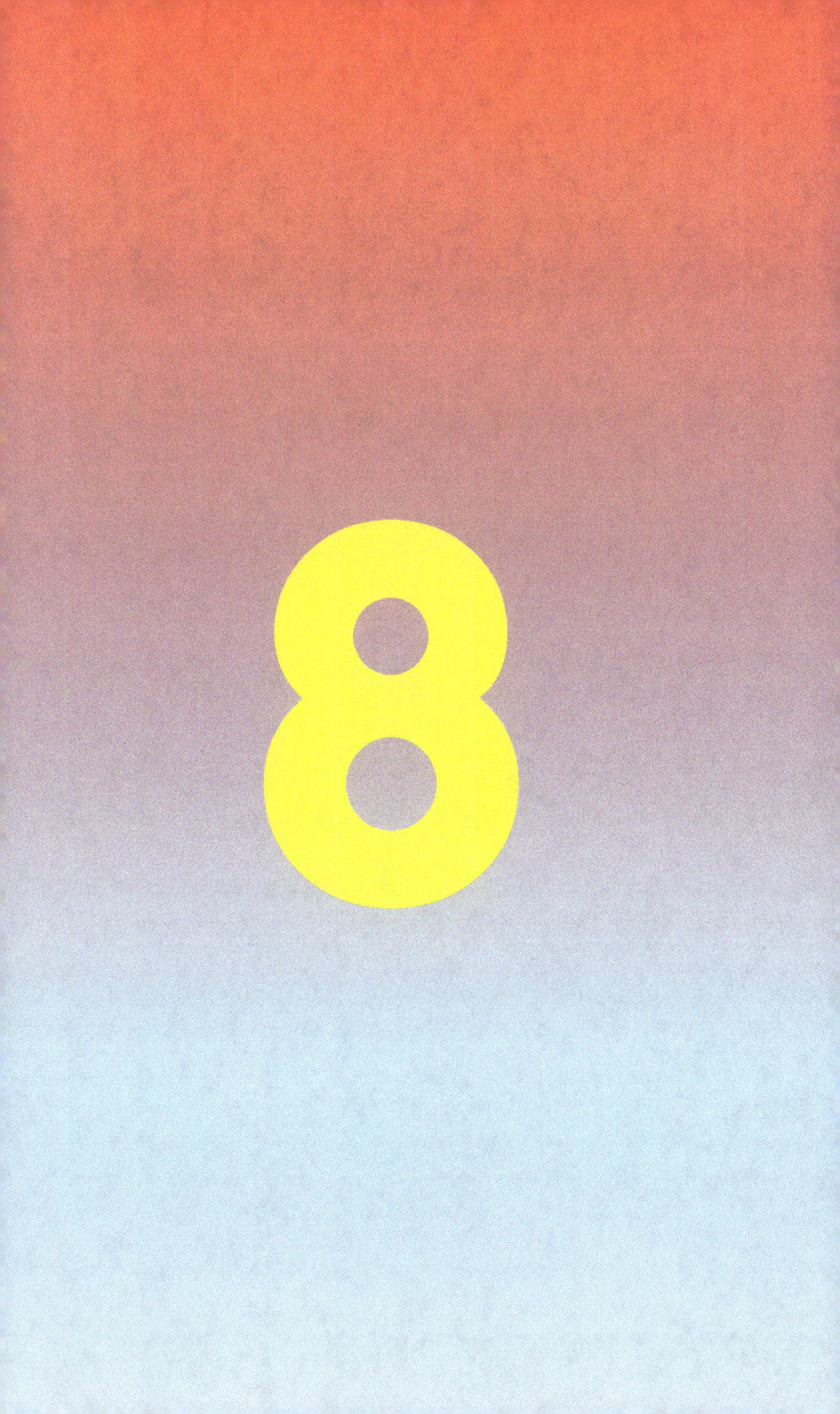

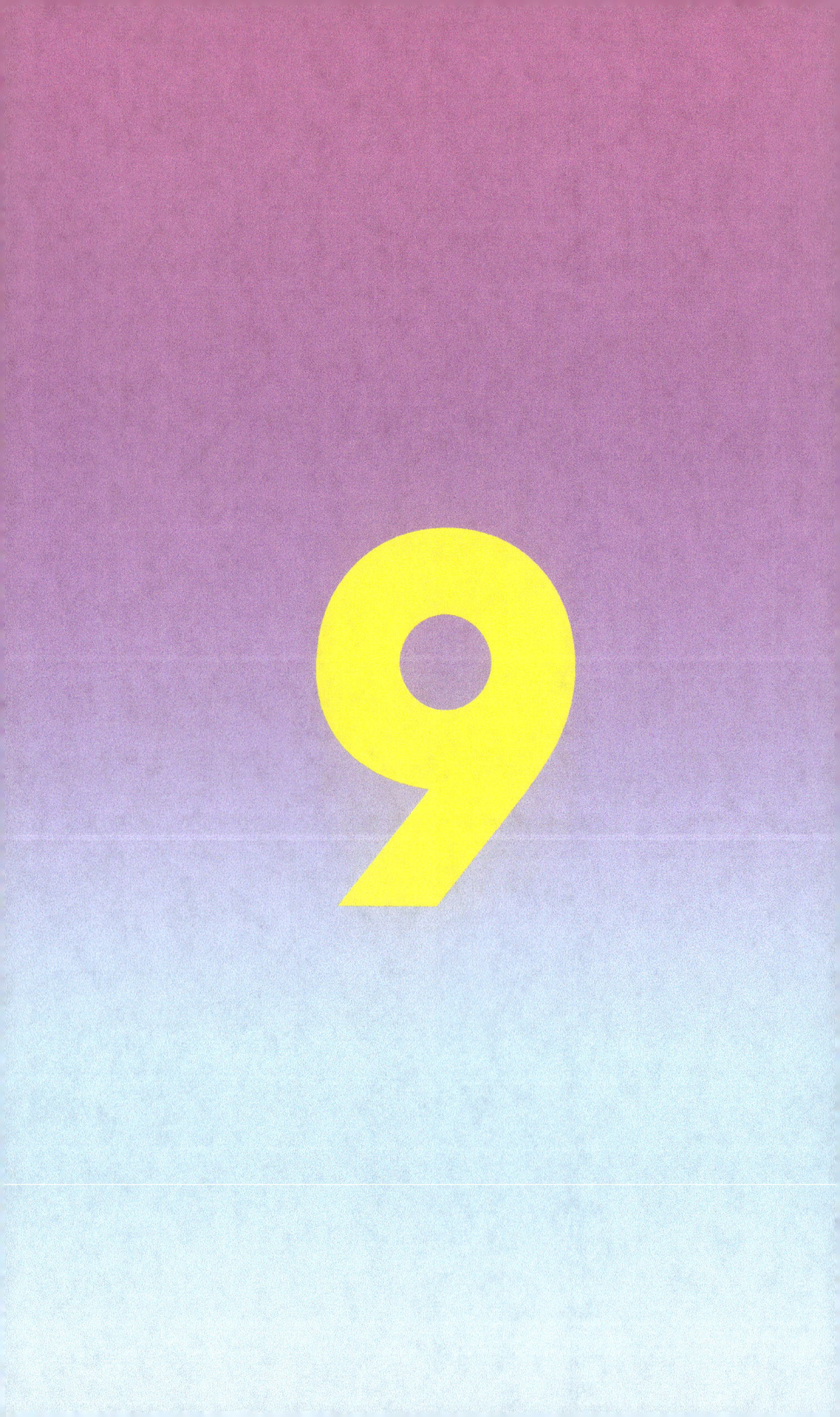

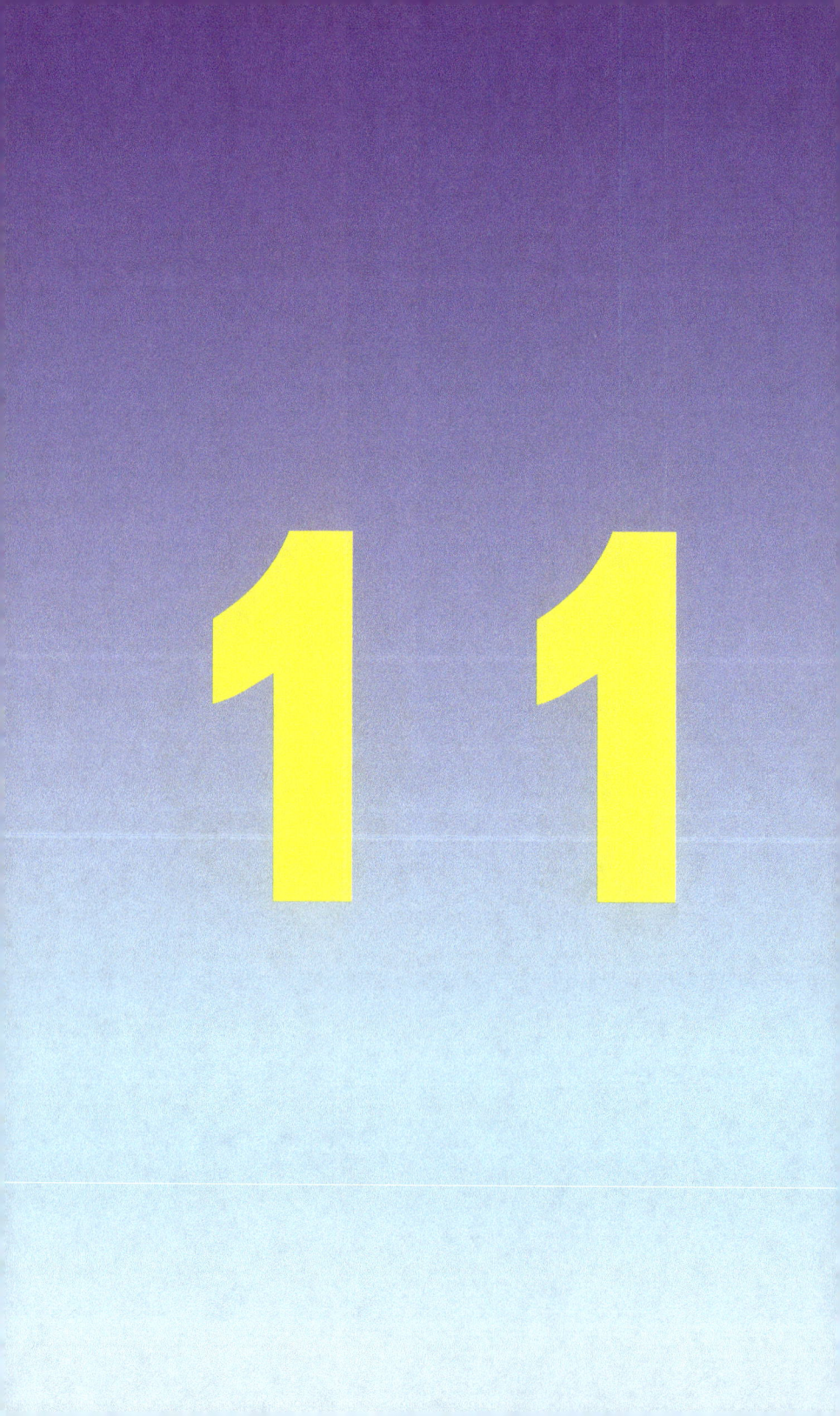

12

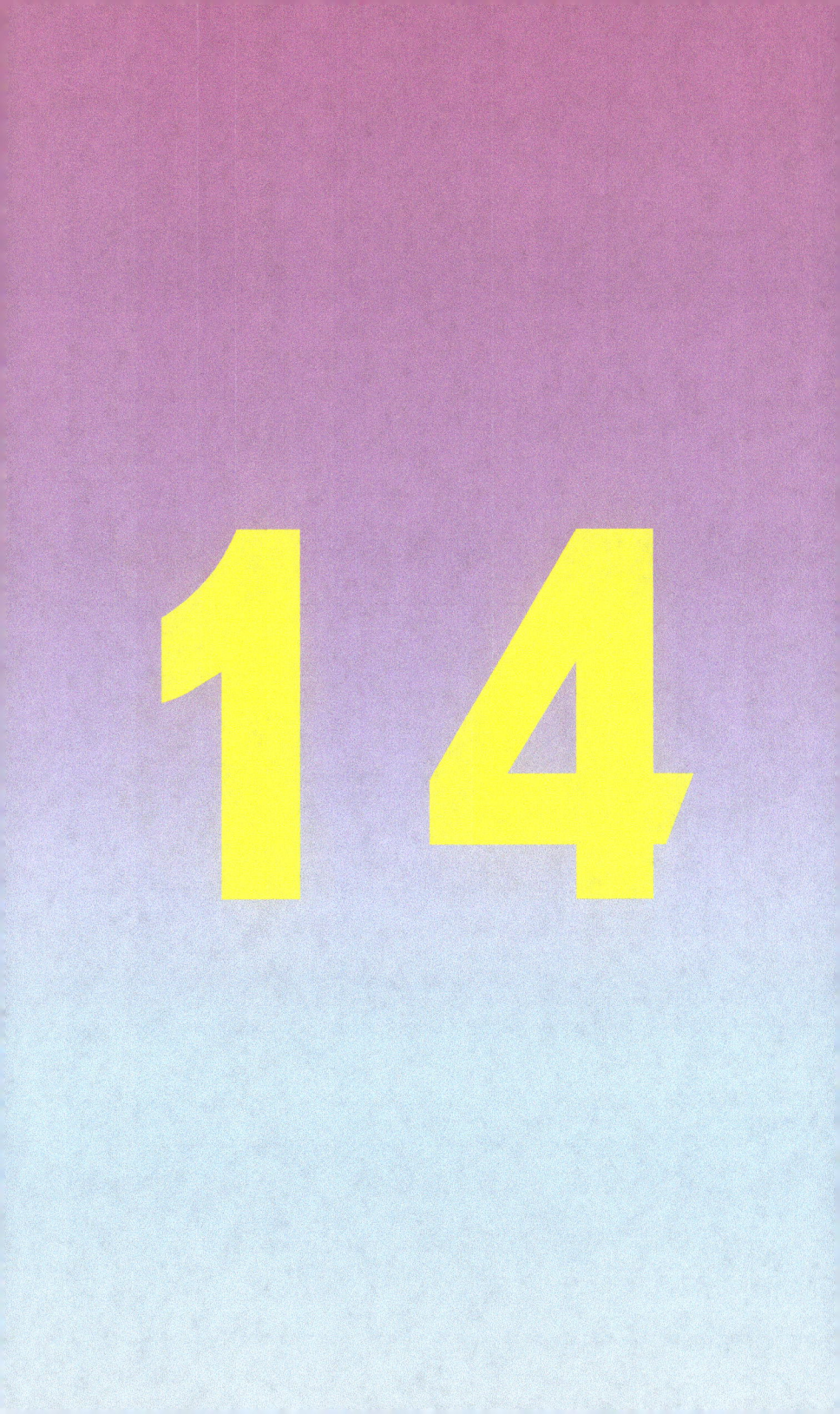

15

16

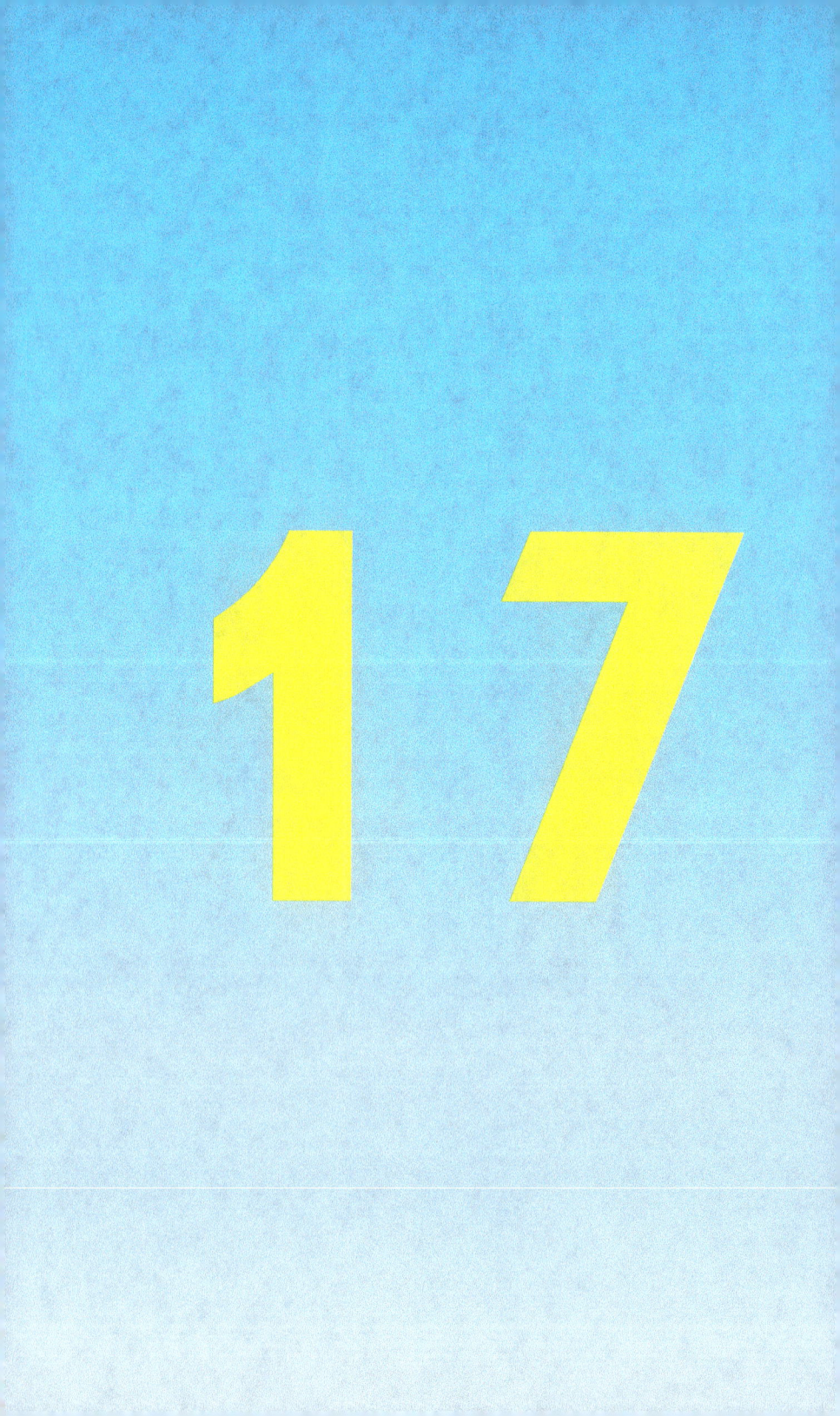

18

19

20